JESUS, REMEMBER ME

JESUS,

REMEMBER ME

WORDS OF ASSURANCE

FROM MARTIN LUTHER

BARBARA OWEN, EDITOR

MINNEAPOLIS

JESUS, REMEMBER ME
Words of Assurance from Martin Luther

Scripture quotations are from the New Revised Standard Version Bible, copyright © 1946, 1952, 1971 by the Division of Christian Education and the National Council of the Churches of Christ in the U.S.A. Used by permission.

Scripture quotations marked TEV are from the Good News Bible (Today's English Version) Old Testament: copyright © 1976 by the American Bible Society; New Testament: copyright © 1966, 1971, 1976 by the American Bible Society. Used by permission.

Cover design by David Meyer
Text design by James Satter

Luther, Martin, 1483-1546.
    [Selections. English. 1998]
    Jesus, remember me : words of assurance from Martin Luther /
Barbara Owen, editor.
      p.   cm.
    Includes bibliographical references.
    ISBN 0-8066-3610-6 (alk. paper)
    1. Theology—Early works to 1800.   2. Christian life—Early works
to 1800. 3. Consolation—Early works to 1800. I. Owen, Barbara,
1935– . II. Title.
BR331.E5094 1998
230'41'092—dc21   98-9838
                                                                CIP

The paper used in this publication meets the minimum requirements of American National Standard for Information Sciences—Permanence of Paper for Printed Library Materials, ANSI Z329.48-1984.

Manufactured in the U.S.A.   AF 9-3610

| 02 | 01 | 00 | 99 | 98 | 1 | 2 | 3 | 4 | 5 | 6 | 7 | 8 | 9 | 10 |

For my husband, Russell

Contents

Introduction

"*Jesus, remember me when you come into your kingdom (Luke 23:42)*," said the thief on the cross next to Jesus. Jesus didn't wait to remember; he responded right then, "Today you will be with me in Paradise."

Often in scripture "remember" means God is about to take action, God has heard prayer, God has not forgotten. To be remembered by God is to receive God's divine help.

In the story of Noah, when the flood is almost over, we read, "But God remembered Noah (Genesis 8:1)." The waters began to subside, and in a few months Noah and his family were living and worshiping on dry land.

"Remember" is used again in the story of Rachel who seemed barren. But "God remembered Rachel, and God heeded her and opened her womb (Genesis 30:22)."

Martin Luther, the sixteenth-century theologian, understood how it was to feel forgotten by God, and he knew the strength of being remembered by God. His life was filled with trials, yet he saw Jesus as his protector and comforter, his savior, and God's chosen one to rescue *humankind and show us what God is like. In his sermons, commentaries, letters, and talks to friends, Luther continually gave assurance that God would not let his people down, no matter how things looked.*

Jesus himself is the assurance of God's never-ending love for people. Martin Luther's vigorous prose still gives this assurance to Christians entering the twenty-first century. In this little book Luther shares words of assurance and hope for troubled times when we may cry, "Jesus, remember me."

Assurance of Faith

There are days when we wonder: Where is God? Why doesn't God answer? Does God really care about me?

Martin Luther knew such doubts. But through his own experience he realized God would forgive him and help him. Pondering how God had helped him in the past could renew Luther's faith. Studying scripture with its many promises of God's love helped. Reading stories of Bible people, such as Noah, gave Luther hope. The temptation to doubt comes to all Christians, but God will strengthen us through such afflictions. Cling to God, Luther says, even when God seems far away.

It is not idle chatter when the Holy Spirit says [in Genesis 8:1] that God remembered Noah and all the animals that were with him in the ark. It indicates that from the day when Noah entered the ark nothing was said to him, nothing was revealed to him, and he saw no ray of grace shining. He clung only to the promise he had received.

It was no joke or laughing matter for Noah and his family and the animals to live shut up in the ark for so long, to see the endless masses of rain, to be tossed about by the waves, and to drift. In these circumstances there was the feeling that God had forgotten them. All their circumstances compelled them to debate whether God was favorably inclined and wanted to remember them. Therefore, although they overcame these hardships, they did not overcome them without awful affliction.

Let us, then, remember that this story sets before us an example of faith, perseverance, and patience, in order that those who have the divine promise may not only learn to believe it but may also realize that they need perseverance.

A person facing the temptation to doubt must by no means rely on himself, nor must he be guided by his own feelings. Rather he must lay hold of the words offered to him in God's name, cling to them, place his trust in them, and direct all the thoughts and feelings of his heart to them.

Second, he must not imagine that he is the only one assailed about his salvation, but he must be aware as, Saint Peter declares, that there are many more people in the world passing through the same trials [1 Peter 5:9].

"We know that tribulation worketh patience, and patience, experience, and experience, hope."

ROMANS 5:3–4

When God wants to strengthen our faith, he first weakens it by feigning to break faith with us. He thrusts us into many tribulations and makes us so weary that we are driven to despair, and yet God gives us strength to be still and persevere.

Such quietness is patience and patience produces experience, so that when God returns to us and lets his sun rise and shine again, and when the storm is over we open our eyes in amazement and say: "The Lord shall be praised, that I have been delivered from evil. God dwells here. I did not think that all would end so well."

Never do people feel the hand of God more closely upon them than when they remember the years of their past life. Here people may see how often they have done and suffered many things without effort or care of their own, yes, even without or against their own will. They gave little thought to them before they occurred or while they were happening. Only after all was over did they find themselves compelled to exclaim in great surprise, "How did these things happen to me, when I gave no thought to them, or thought something very different?" Here we see how often God was with us when we neither saw nor sensed it.

Therefore, even if there were no books or sermons, our very own lives, led through so many evils and dangers, would, if considered properly, abundantly commend to us the ever present and most tender goodness of God, which, far beyond our thought and feeling, carried us in its bosom.

In his true form God is a God who loves the afflicted, has mercy upon the humbled, forgives the fallen, and revives the drooping. How can any more pleasant picture be painted of God? God is favorably disposed to us even when we seem to ourselves to be forsaken and distressed.

God, O God? Do you not hear me, my God? Are you dead? No, you cannot die; you are merely hiding yourself. O God, stand by me in the name of your dear Son, Jesus Christ, who shall be my Protector and Defender, yes, my mighty Fortress, through the might and the strengthening of your Holy Spirit.

People either smugly despise and hate the word and promises of God or, when they do hear them, say they doubt and do not know whether God is so merciful, whether he favorably hears and cares for those who call upon him, especially the unworthy and poor sinners.

But when a heart is in such doubt, it may very quickly be driven even to blasphemy and despair. This is why Saint Paul so frequently exhorts us to have full assurance, that is a firm and immovable recognition of God's will toward us, which gives assurance to our consciences and steels them against doubt and unbelief.

"For God so loved the world that he gave his only Son, so that everyone who believes in him may not perish but may have eternal life."

JOHN 3:16

The person who has only a tiny drop or spark of spiritual trust should know that it is a blessing of God and an exceptional gift. For if we could firmly and indubitably believe God's promises, our hearts would be imbued with a strength far too great to be frightened by the world or the devil or all the gates of hell.

Therefore the words of the oaths and promises of God must be diligently pondered. God exhorts us as a most gracious Father, he urges us, he presses us in whichever way he can. God promises, he offers himself as a pledge—all for the sole purpose that we may believe him.

The twofold armor with which the devil is slain and at which he is afraid is first: to hearken unceasingly to the word of God, to instruct oneself in it, and to be comforted and strengthened by it. And second, when temptation and struggle come upon us, to lift up our hearts to that self-same word, and cry to God, invoking him for help.

Hence one of two things is always present, continuing as an eternal conversation between God and the soul. Either God speaks to us and we are still, listening to God, or God listens to us as we speak to him, praying for what we need.

"Whatever you ask for in prayer, believe that you have received it, and it will be yours."

MARK 11:24

We must reflect on this promise and remind God of it, and in that way be emboldened to pray with confidence. But your trust must not set a goal for God, not set a time and place, not specify the way or the means of his fulfillment. It must entrust all of that to God's will, wisdom, and omnipotence. Just wait cheerfully and undauntedly for the fulfillment.

God's divine wisdom will find an immeasurably better way and method, time and place, than we can imagine. We must acknowledge that we are too paltry to be able to mention such things. All this we must leave entirely to the discretion of God and most firmly believe that he will hear us.

The highest of all God's commands is this, that we hold up before our eyes the image of his dear Son, our Lord Jesus Christ. Every day he should be our excellent mirror wherein we behold how much God loves us and how well, in his infinite goodness, he has cared for us in that he gave his dear Son for us.

Turn away from your doubts and contemplate the brazen serpent, that is, Christ given for us. Then, God willing, you will feel better.

Why, then, does God let such suffering and affliction befall those whom he loves most?

First, because God wants to save his people from pride, so that the great saints who have received such special grace from him should not venture to put their trust in themselves. Therefore it must be thus mingled and salted for them that they do not always possess the power of the Spirit, but that, at times, their faith grows restless and their hearts faint, so that they perceive what they are and confess that they can achieve nothing unless the pure grace of God sustains them.

Assurance of Forgiveness

Martin Luther understood that the forgiveness of God makes saints out of sinners. It is an ongoing process—we are always sinners being made saints. This process is God's work in us; God's continuing forgiveness frees us from the necessity of winning our own salvation.

And so, Luther reminds us, God's continuing forgiveness frees us to use our time and energies in caring for other people. This forgiveness enables us to forgive others, too.

I see a long list of my sins. And yet I am not to look at these sins; I am to act as if I had never committed them. Hence there is no other way to acquire the remission of sins but by closing my eyes and believing that my sins are forgiven.

As yet I have not mastered the art of doing this, but I am learning it. We who are interested have a hard time learning to appreciate what Christ's forgiveness is, for the habit of wanting to wipe out our sins through efforts of our own clings to us forever.

The Holy Scriptures call Christians saints and the people of God. It's a pity that it's forgotten that we are saints, for to forget this is to forget Christ and baptism.

You say that the sins which we commit every day offend God, and therefore we are not saints. To this I reply: Mother love is stronger than the filth and scabbiness on a child, and so the love of God toward us is stronger than the dirt that clings to us. Accordingly, although we are sinners, we do not lose our filial relation on account of our filthiness, nor do we fall from grace on account of our sin.

Only those sinners belong in the kingdom of Christ who recognize their sin, feel it, and then catch hold of the word of Christ: "I do not condemn you." These people constitute the membership of Christ's kingdom. He does not admit those who think they are without sin.

But if sinners enter, they do not remain sinners. Christ spreads his cloak over them, saying: "If you have fallen into sin, I forgive you and cover your sin." To be sure, sin is there. But the Lord in this kingdom closes his eyes to it. He covers it over, forgives it, and does not count it against you.

Thus you are made a living saint and a true member of Christ.

"Likewise the Spirit helps us in our weakness."
ROMANS 8:26

Let no one think that he will be freed from all sin, lust, and evil thoughts. Each must continue to yearn for such freedom and cry to God: "Ah, if only I could be set free from sin." The voice of the Holy Spirit will thus cry in us till the Last Day.

Therefore sin always abides in us poor Christians. We fall into sin, but not willfully or out of wickedness, but from weakness, which God can well forgive.

Therefore it is the best comfort that we have the testimony of the Holy Spirit within us. This means that when we are in need and cry to God, he will be gracious to us and will help us. We can trust in God and know that he will not forsake us, and thus we show that we are truly Christians.

I remember that Staupitz [Luther's friend and one-time superior] used to say: "More than a thousand times I have vowed to God that I would improve, but I have never performed what I have vowed. Hereafter I shall not make such vows, because I know perfectly well that I shall not live up to them. Unless God is gracious and merciful to me for the sake of Christ and grants me a blessed final hour, I shall not be able to stand before him with all my vows and good works." This despair is not only truthful but is godly and holy. Whoever wants to be saved must make this confession with the mouth and with the heart.

Christ has not freed us from human duties, but from eternal wrath. Where? In the conscience. That is the limit of our freedom, and it must go no further. For Christ has set us spiritually free, that is, he has set us free in the sense that our conscience is free and joyful and no longer fears the coming wrath of God.

That is true freedom, and no one can value it high enough. For who can express what a great thing it is that you are certain that God is no longer angry with you and will never be angry again, but for the sake of Christ is now, and ever will be, a gracious and merciful Father. Truly, it is a wonderful freedom above all understanding, that God's high Majesty is gracious unto us.

"For if you forgive others their trespasses, your heavenly Father will also forgive you."

MATTHEW 6:14

Think how you would like it if God should do unto you as you do to your neighbor, and should expose all your sin to the world? Or how should you like it if some other person would make known all your malice? You would doubtless want everyone to be silent, to excuse you and cover up your evil and pray for you. Thus the Lord says also, "In everything do to others as you would have them do to you (Matthew 7:12)."

The love of the Son of God for us is of such magnitude that the greater the filth and stench of our sins, the more he befriends us, the more he cleanses us, relieving us of all our misery and of the burden of all our sins and placing them upon his own back.

Whenever the devil declares: "You are a sinner!" Christ interposes: "I will reverse the order; I will be a sinner, and you are to go scot-free." Who can thank our God enough for this mercy?

*"Guard the doors of your mouth from her
who lies in your embrace."*

MICAH 7:5

Here the prophet does not want suspicion and hatred to exist between spouses. He wants the utmost love and good will which cannot exist without mutual trust. And yet he wants a limit to this trust, because it can happen that it is mistaken. For your spouse is a human being. Although this spouse fears God and pays heed to his word, nevertheless, because Satan, the enemy, is lying in wait everywhere and because human nature is weak, your spouse can fall and disappoint your hope somewhere.

When you foresee this with your mind, you will be readier to forgive, and you will be less distressed if anything happens contrary to what you had hoped. Thus love will remain, and harmony will not be disturbed. For nothing has happened that was not anticipated, and love is readiest to forgive. This is indeed a rare gift, but because you are a Christian, remember that this ought to be your attitude.

Christian freedom may be enjoyed both by one who is free and by one who is a bondsman, by one who is a captive and by one who takes others captive, by a woman as well as a man, by a servant and a maid as well as by a lord and a lady. We are speaking of the freedom before God, the freedom we have when God pronounces us free from sin. This freedom is extended to all.

May our dear Lord Jesus Christ show you his hands and his side and gladden your heart with his love, and may you behold and hear only him until you find your joy in him. Amen.

Some will say with false humility: God forbid that any Christians should be so presumptuous as to allow themselves to be called saints! Are we not all sinners?

Answer: All such thoughts spring from the old illusion that when sanctity is mentioned, people think of mighty deeds. They look to the saints in heaven, as if they themselves had won and merited their position.

But we say that the true saints of Christ must be good strong sinners and remain such saints as are not ashamed to pray the Lord's Prayer. They are called holy, not because they are without sin, or sanctified through works. On the contrary, they are sinners in themselves and are condemned with all their works. But they are made saints with a sanctity which is not their own, but Christ the Lord's, which is given to them through faith and becomes their own.

Assurance in Illness

Illness was a very present fact of life in the sixteenth century. The plague swept over Europe at various times during Martin Luther's life. Although he was spared this disease, he suffered many other illnesses and health problems. Luther and his wife Katie cared for many sick people in their home. Even so, in his writings Luther may not seem as sympathetic as we would like. For us, illness is a jarring interruption in our life.

In the sixteenth century, illness was perhaps more expected and seen as part of life than it is today. Yet Luther saw God providing care through medicines, physicians, pastors, and others. He encouraged people to recognize that God does care for the sick.

Luther also urged people to adopt healthy habits of sleep, diet, and exercise. He himself was fond of bowling and said, "Moving about produces health; and health makes one move about." His friends noted, though, that he didn't always practice what he preached in regards to a healthy lifestyle. His words about health were perhaps to remind himself as well as others to take care of the body. Take care of yourself, take care of each other, pray, and know that God is with you, Luther tells us.

The two names for the Holy Spirit, "Comforter" and "Spirit of Truth," are very affectionate and consoling names. This, says Christ, shall be the office of the Holy Spirit when I have left you. The Holy Spirit shall be your Comforter— when you shall find no comfort nor support in the world, when all the world shall be against you, when the devil shall beset you with melancholy and gloomy thoughts of your own infirmities, so that you might well despair if you were left in that state without comfort and strength.

But, says Christ, to protect you against this slanderer and accuser, the devil, I will send you, from my Father and in my stead, the Holy Spirit, who shall be your counselor and defender, and who shall intercede for you before God. He shall comfort and strengthen your hearts, so that you need not despair.

Let your heart be strong and at ease in your trouble, for we have yonder a true mediator with God, Jesus Christ. He has said, promised, and pledged this. He will not and cannot lie; of that we are certain. "Ask," says he, "and it shall be given you; seek, and ye shall find; knock, and it shall be opened unto you [Matthew 7:7]."

And the whole Psalter is full of such comforting promises, especially Psalm 91, which is particularly good to read to the sick.

"Into your hand I commit my spirit."

PSALM 31:5

This passage I learned, in my sickness, to correct; in the first translation, I applied it only to the hour of death: but it should be said: My health, my happiness, my life, misfortune, sickness, death, etc., stand all in thy hands. Experience testifies this.

If someone wants the chaplain or pastor to come, let the sick person send word in time to call him and let him do so early enough while he is still in his right mind before illness overwhelms the patient. The reason I say this is that some are so negligent that they make no request and send no message until the soul is perched for flight on the tip of their tongues and they are no longer rational or able to speak.

Then we are told, "Dear Sir, say the very best you can to him." But earlier, when the illness first began, they wanted no visit from the pastor, but would say, "Oh, there's no need. I hope he'll get better." How can a diligent pastor serve such people?

God employs means for the preservation of health, such as sleep, food, and drink, for he does nothing except through instruments.

Our Lord God created all things, and they are good. Wherefore it's permissible to use medicine, for it is a creature of God.

Thus I replied to [John] Hohndorf [the mayor of Wittenberg], who inquired of me when he heard that it's not permissible to make use of medicine. I said to him, "Do you eat when you're hungry?"

Some people sin in that they are much too rash and reckless, tempting God and disregarding everything which might counteract death and the plague. They disdain the use of medicines; they do not avoid places and persons infected by the plague, but lightheartedly make sport of it and wish to prove how independent they are. They say that it is God's punishment; if he wants to protect them he can do so without medicines or our carefulness.

This is not trusting God but tempting him. God has created medicines and provided us with intelligence to guard and take good care of the body so that we can live in good health.

[To Philip Melanchthon, a friend and colleague whom Luther felt was in danger of overtaxing his physical and nervous strength by overworking "for the glory of God."]

I command you and the entire circle of my friends to force you, under the threat of an anathema, to observe regular habits for the sake of your health so that you do not commit suicide [by overwork] and then pretend you did it in obedience to God. For we also serve God by doing nothing, in fact, in no way more than by doing nothing. For this reason God, above all things, wanted the Sabbath so rigidly kept. See to it that you do not despise this.

I expect that exercise and change of air do more good than all their purgings and bleedings, but when we do employ medical remedies, we should be careful to do so under the advice of a judicious physician.

A physician is our Lord God's mender of the body, as we theologians are his healers of the spirit.

To my dear father, John Luther,

My brother James has written me that you are seriously ill. As the weather is bad and the season dangerous, I am very anxious about you for though God has given you a strong, tough body, yet your age and the inclemency of the weather give me disquieting thoughts. None of us is, or should be, sure of his life at any time.

I pray from the bottom of my heart that our Father, who has made you my father, will strengthen you according to his immeasurable kindness and enlighten and protect you with his Spirit, so that you may receive with joy and thanksgiving the blessed teaching of his Son, our Lord Jesus Christ.

May our dear Lord and Savior be with you so that, God willing, we may see each other, either here or yonder. For our faith is certain, and we doubt not that we shall shortly see each other in the presence of Christ. Our departure from life is a smaller thing to God than my journey would be from here to Mansfeld or yours from Mansfeld to Wittenberg. It is only an hour's sleep, and after that all will be different. This is most certainly true.

A sound regimen produces excellent effects. When I feel indisposed, by observing a strict diet and going to bed early, I generally manage to get round again, that is if I can keep my mind tolerably at rest.

Dear Cordatus [a pastor friend of Luther]:

I thank God that your health is being restored. But I pray you to curb your suspicion that you are assailed by who knows how many diseases. You know the proverb, "Imagination produces misfortune." Therefore, you ought to take the pains to divert rather than to entertain such notions.

I too must do this. For our adversary, the devil, walks about, seeking not only to devour our souls but also to weaken our bodies with thoughts of our souls in the hope that he might perhaps slay our bodies. He knows that our physical health depends in large measure on the thoughts in our minds. This is in accord with the saying, "Good cheer is half the battle," and, "A cheerful heart is a good medicine, but a downcast spirit dries up the bones [Proverbs 17:22]." I give you this advice although I confess that I do not take it myself.

"Trust in him at all times, O people;
pour out your heart before him;
God is a refuge for us."

PSALM 62:8

If you are lacking something, well, here is good advice: "Pour out your heart before him." Voice your complaint freely, and do not conceal anything from God. Regardless of what it is, just throw it in a pile before him, as you open your heart completely to a good friend. God wants to hear it, and he wants to give you his aid and counsel. Do not be bashful before God, and do not think that what you ask is too big or too much. Come right out with it, even if all you have is bags full of need. Do not dribble your requests before him. The more you ask, the happier God is to hear you. Only pour it all out, do not dribble or drip it. For God will not drip or dribble either, but he will flood you with a veritable deluge.

Assurance in Anxiety

Martin Luther knew from experience what it was to be despondent and anxious. He had bouts with this all his life. He developed remedies which he shared with others, often through letters of consolation and encouragement.

In Luther's years as a monk he had spent much time alone and he knew how melancholy thoughts—and, in his view, the devil—could plague one in times of solitude. He suggested one get out and be with friends, use music, sports, meals together, Bible reading, and prayer all as remedies for anxiety and despondency. He saw such remedies as God's good gifts to us; we should use them, giving thanks to God.

But if you can't avoid solitude, then, as Luther biographer Roland H. Bainton notes, Luther suggests that you go "out to the fields and spread the manure: do something downright earthy."

Luther's empathy with those going through such anxious or despondent times is real and heartfelt. He even readily admits that he still has trouble taking his own advice. But God is with us, no matter what, and God's Spirit intercedes for us.

[To a dejected young prince.]

I should like to encourage Your Grace, who are a young man, always to be joyful, to engage in riding and hunting, and to seek the company of others who may be able to rejoice with Your Grace in a godly and honorable way. For solitude and melancholy are poisonous.

Your Grace has Master Nicholas Hausmann and many others near at hand. Be merry with them; for gladness and good cheer, when decent and proper, are the best medicine for a young person—indeed, for all people. I myself, who have spent a good part of my life in sorrow and gloom, now seek and find pleasure wherever I can. Praise God, we now have sufficient understanding [of the word of God] to be able to rejoice with a good conscience and to use God's gifts with thanksgiving, for he created them for this purpose and is pleased when we use them.

Be merry, then, both inwardly in Christ himself and outwardly in his gifts and the good things of life. He will have it so. It is for this that he is with us. It is for this that he provides his gifts—that we may use them and be glad, and that we may praise, love, and thank him forever.

When one's spirit busies itself with oppressive thinking, then sleeping, eating, and digesting are impaired; for when the spirit is dispirited, the body must suffer for it. For all emotions and passions that are excessive exhaust the body. The body without the spirit is dead; it is a horse without a rider. But a quiet spirit preserves the body. Therefore oppressive thinking is to be resisted as much as possible. My most strenuous struggle consists in fighting oppressive thoughts.

[To the reverend gentleman in Christ, Mr. John Schlaginhaufen, faithful minister of the word: grace and peace in Christ.]

Thank you for the medlars you sent me. I like these native fruits better than the ones imported from Italy. If they are somewhat harsh to the taste, at least they are ripe.

I am sorry to hear that you are still depressed at times. Christ is as near to you as you are to yourself, and he will not harm you, for he shed his blood for you. Dear friend, honor this good, faithful man. Believe that he esteems and loves you more than does Dr. Luther or any other Christian. What you expect of us, expect even more of him. Herewith I commit you and yours to God's keeping. Amen.

*"Cast your burden on the Lord,
and he will sustain you."*

PSALM 55:22

Whoever desires to be a Christian must learn to believe this verse, and to exercise this faith in all affairs, in physical and in spiritual things, in doing and in suffering, in living and dying, and to cast aside all anxious thoughts and cares and throw them cheerfully off. Yet this person must not throw them into a corner, as some have vainly tried to do. These cares will not let themselves be stripped of their power so long as they are allowed to dwell in the heart.

But you must cast both your heart and your care upon God's back, for he has a strong neck and shoulders, and can well carry them. And, moreover, he bids us cast them upon him, and the more we cast on him, the more he is pleased, for he promises that he will bear your burden for you, and everything that concerns you. "Cast ye all your care upon him; for he careth for you."

Dear Matthias,

Do not dwell on your own thoughts, but listen to what people have to say to you. For God has commanded Christians to comfort one another, and it is God's will that the afflicted should receive such consolation as God's very own. Our Lord also commanded us not to be anxious, but to cast our cares upon him, for he careth for us, as Saint Peter [1 Peter 5:7] taught from Psalm 55:22.

Listen, then, to what we are saying to you in God's name: Rejoice in Christ, who is your gracious Lord and Redeemer. Let him bear your burdens, for he assuredly cares for you, even if you do not yet have all that you would like. He still lives. Look to him for the best.

Solitude produces melancholy. When we are alone, the worst and saddest things come to mind. We reflect in detail upon all sorts of evils. And if we have encountered adversity in our lives, we dwell upon it as much as possible, magnify it, think that no one is so unhappy as we are, and imagine the worst possible consequences.

In short, when we are alone, we think of one thing and another, we leap to conclusions, and we interpret everything in the worst light. On the other hand, we imagine that other people are very happy, and it distresses us that things go well with them and evil with us.

When Christ was wrestling with temptation in the garden (Matthew 26:37 ff.), we see him seeking comfort among his three disciples. When Paul, in Acts 28:15, saw the believers coming to meet him, he took courage from the sight and experienced comfort. Loneliness distresses a person who is solitary and deprived of intimate friends. He can exert himself and struggle against it, but he does not overcome it without great difficulty.

Everything is less burdensome if you have a faithful friend with you; for then the promise applies (Matthew 18:20): "Where two or three are gathered in my name, there am I in the midst of them." Therefore solitude should be shunned and the companionship of familiar people sought, especially in spiritual perils.

[To Luther's friend and colleague Philip Melanchthon.]

With all my heart I hate those cares by which you state that you are consumed. If your cause is true, why should we make Christ a liar when he has given us such great promises and commands us to be confident and undismayed? "Cast thy burden upon the Lord," he says. "The Lord is nigh unto all them that call upon him." Does he speak like this for nothing, or to beasts?

I too am sometimes downcast, but not all the time. What good do you expect to accomplish by these vain worries of yours? I pray for you very earnestly, and I am deeply pained that you keep sucking up cares like a leech and thus rendering my prayers vain.

May Christ comfort all of you by his Spirit and strengthen and instruct you. Amen.

[To a nobleman given to bouts of melancholy thought.]

If you do not resist and oppose such thoughts, but rather give them free reign to torment you, the battle will soon be lost.

But the best counsel of all is this: Do not struggle against your thoughts at all, but ignore them and act as if you were not conscious of them. Think constantly of something else, and say: "Well, devil, do not trouble me. I have no time for your thoughts. I must eat, drink, ride, go, or do this or that."

Then undertake to do anything else that you are able—whether play or something else—just so that you free yourself from these thoughts, hold them in contempt, and dismiss them. If necessary, speak coarsely and disrespectfully, like this: "Dear devil, if you can't do better than that, kiss my toe, etc. I have no time for you now."

In addition, our prayers and those of all godly Christians should and will also help you.

Whenever a person in fear of death cries unto God, God cannot refrain from helping him. Christ did not stay long outside the room where his frightened disciples were hiding after the crucifixion and resurrection, but soon was there comforting them and saying: "Peace be unto you," and "I am come, be of good cheer and fear not." So it is still. When we are afraid, God lifts us up and causes the gospel to be preached to us, and thus restores to us a glad and sure conscience.

[To a friend with musical gifts.]

When you are sad and when melancholy threatens to get the upper hand, say: "Arise! I must play a song unto the Lord on my regal [a portable organ], for the Scriptures teach us that it pleases him to hear a joyful song and the music of stringed instruments." Then begin striking the keys and singing in accompaniment, as David and Elisha did, until your sad thoughts vanish.

If the devil returns and plants worries and sad thoughts in your mind, resist him again and say, "Begone, devil! I must now play and sing unto my Lord Christ."

"You are the most handsome of men; grace is poured upon your lips."

PSALM 45:2

The psalmist has diligently read the prophecies and promises regarding Christ and has seen that his lips are the sweetest and loveliest lips, which attract the hearts of all the weak.

Grace is on the lips of this King. Not only that, it overflows, so that you may understand how abundantly this fountain of grace flows and gushes forth. As though the psalmist said: "Our King has wisdom such as no one has, namely, the sweetest and loveliest wisdom. He helps the penitent, comforts the afflicted, recalls the despairing, raises up the fallen and humiliated, justifies sinners, gives life to the dying."

Therefore this King says in Isaiah 50:4: "The Lord has given me the tongue of those who are taught," that is, the Lord has given me a fluent tongue, "that I may know how to sustain with a word the one that is weary."

Assurance of Purpose

Why are we here? What is our purpose in life? In the Middle Ages a religious vocation was considered the highest service to God. But Martin Luther saw things differently. He saw all vocations and stations in life as meaningful before God. Changing a diaper, working in the fields, ruling a kingdom are all services done to the glory of God if the person understands this as a calling.

Luther also sees a primary purpose of our lives being that of prayer. Christians serve themselves, their neighbors, their country and the world through their prayers.

Further, Luther understood that we love God by caring for and loving other people, especially the weak, the poor, and the needy. God gives us gifts and talents. With these, God works through us for other people. Luther speaks of God working in hidden ways in the world. He calls these hidden ways "masks" of God. God hides himself in our works which we do for others, using the gifts God has given us.

God needs many and various offices and stations for people. Therefore God bestows many different kinds of gifts and so contrives things that we always need one another. What would princes, nobles, and regents be if there were not others, such as pastors, preachers, teachers, farmers, craftsmen, and the like? They would not and could not learn or do everything alone and by themselves.

All God's people live by the same Spirit and by the same faith, and are guided and governed by the same Spirit and the same faith. But they all do different external works. For God does not work through them at the same time, in the same place, in the same work, or in the sight of the same people. God moves at different times, in different places, in different works and in different people, but God always rules them by the same Spirit and in the same faith.

So that his ways may be hidden and his footsteps unrecognizable [Psalm 77:19], God provides each one with other works in other times and places, just as he did with other saints. And each one is compelled by the work, place, time, persons, and circumstances, previously unknown to him, to follow God as he rules and guides him.

This is the true knowledge of faith in which all God's people are instructed, each one in his own vocation.

Every person surely has a calling. While attending to it, each person serves God. Therefore it is a great wisdom when human beings do what God commands and earnestly devote themselves to their vocations without taking into consideration what others are doing.

But surely there are few who do this. The layman longs for the life of a cleric, the pupil wishes to be a teacher, the citizen wants to be a councilor, and each one of us loathes our own calling, although there is no other way of serving God than to walk in simple faith and then to stick diligently to one's calling and to keep a good conscience.

If God wants to do something extraordinary through you, he will call you and will point out opportunities. Avail yourself of them. If this does not happen, you may nevertheless rejoice that you are in a divine calling when you assume and perform the ordinary duties of this life such as sowing, plowing, building.

When a maid milks the cows or a hired man hoes the field—provided that they are believers, namely, that they conclude that this kind of life is pleasing to God and was instituted by God—they truly serve God.

What is our work in field and garden, in town and house, in war and in government, to God, but the work of children, by which God wants to give his gifts in the fields, at home, and everywhere? Our works are masks of God, behind which God wants to remain hidden, although he does all things.

We have the saying: "God gives every good thing, but not just by waving a wand." God gives all good gifts, but you must lend a hand and take the bull by the horns. That is, you must work and thus give God good cause and a mask.

Through prayer Christians obtain for themselves and for others all that they ask of God, even physical things. This is one of the greatest works they do to help and preserve the world, even if they did nothing else.

And we, as Christians, must know that the whole system of earthly government stands and remains for its allotted time solely through God's order or command and the prayers of Christians. These are the two pillars that support the entire world.

If you are powerful, it is not that you may make the weak weaker by oppression, but that you may make them powerful by raising them up and defending them. You are wise, not in order to laugh at the foolish and thereby make them more foolish, but that you may undertake to teach them as you yourself would wish to be taught. You are righteous that you may vindicate and pardon the unrighteous, not that you may only condemn, disparage, judge, and punish.

"You shall love the Lord your God with all your heart . . . and your neighbor as yourself."

There you have the good works described all together. These we should practice toward one another as our heavenly Father has done toward us and is still doing unceasingly. You have often heard that we need no works to please God, but we need them for our neighbor. We cannot make God any more powerful or richer through our works, but we can make our neighbor stronger and richer by them. Our neighbor needs our works, and they should be directed toward the neighbor and not to God.

My faith I must bring inwardly and upwards to God, but my works I must do outwardly and downward to my neighbor.

> *"Each of us must please our neighbor for the good purpose of building up the neighbor."*
>
> ROMANS 15:2

A Christian lives for one purpose only, namely, to do good to others, and not to destroy them but their vices. One cannot do this unless one is willing to have to do with the weak. It would be a foolish work of charity if you feed the hungry, give drink to the thirsty, clothe the naked, visit the sick, but would not suffer the hungry, naked, sick, and thirsty to visit you and be in your company. And if you would not suffer the wicked and the frail to be with you, that would be the same as saying that you did not wish to help one soul to sanctity.

Therefore let us learn from this Epistle that the Christian way of living does not consist in finding saintly, righteous, and holy people, but in making them. And let this be the Christian's work and practice on earth, to make such people, whether by punishment, or prayer, or by suffering for them, or in whatever way they can. Likewise, a Christian lives not to find rich, strong, and healthy people, but to make the poor, the weak, and sick, rich, strong, and healthy.

We have been ordained through God to the priestly office. Hence we can and must step before God joyfully, as we bring both our own need and that of others before him, assured by his promise that our prayers will be heard and that he will say yea and amen to them.

". . . just as you did it to one of the least of these
who are members of my family, you did it to me."

Who could ever have discerned that God lets himself come so low, that he receives all these works which we do to the poor and needy as if they had been done to him? Thus the world is full of God. In every yard, in every lane you may find Christ. Do not gaze up into the sky and say: "If I could but once see our Lord God, how readily I should render him any service in my power!"

Listen—do you wish to serve God? You have him in your home, with your servants and children; teach them to fear God and put their trust in him alone, and love him. Go and comfort your sad and sick neighbors, help them with all your possessions, wisdom, and skill. Bring up your children that they may know Christ, give them a good and saintly schoolmaster; spare no cost with them. God shall reward you richly.

Christ says: "See that you do not fail to see me. I shall be close to you in every poor and wretched person, who is in need of your help and teaching; I am there, right in the midst. Whether you do little for that person or much, you do it unto me."

"This is my commandment,
that you love one another as I have loved you."
JOHN 15:12

It is natural—and everybody must admit this—that everyone would like to be shown love, fidelity, and help. Therefore we have been intermingled by God in order that we may live side by side and serve and help one another. God has no need whatever of such service and help, nor does Christ give this command for his sake. But we, of course, need it in our inmost hearts.

Assurance of Abundance

Sometimes Christians of modest or abundant means are anxious because of their wealth. What should they think about this wealth?

Whether we are rich in money and material goods or we are poor in these things, Martin Luther assures us that our greatest abundance comes from God in our baptism and salvation. While Luther was not rich himself, he did not think having money was evil. He saw worldly goods and money as gifts from God to be used for God's work in the world.

Luther would assure rich Christians today that it is all right to be wealthy if one gives thanks to God, and then not only enjoys the wealth but uses it for the good of others. "Possessions belong in your hands, not in your heart," he says.

Now we have received from God nothing but love and favor, for Christ has pledged and given us his righteousness and everything he has. He has poured out upon us all his treasures, which no mortal can measure and no angel can understand or fathom, for God is a glowing furnace of love, reaching even from the earth to the heavens.

The apostles Peter and Paul differentiate between brotherly love and love in general. Brotherhood means that Christians should all be like brothers and sisters and make no distinction among them. Since we all have one Christ in common, one Baptism, one faith, one treasure, I am no better than you are. For what you have I also have, and I am just as rich as you are.

Thus in Baptism we Christians have all obtained one brotherhood. From this no saint has more than I and you. For I have been bought with just as high a price as he has been bought. God has spent just as much on me as he has spent on the greatest saint.

To put it very briefly, God does not want us to serve money and possessions. Nor does he want us to worry. But God does want us to work and leave the worry to him. Let the one who has possessions be the master of these possessions. The one who serves is a servant and does not have the possessions; the possessions have him. For he dare not use them when he wants to; nor does he dare serve others with them. In fact, he is not bold enough to touch the stuff.

But if he is master of the possessions, the possessions serve him, and he does not serve them. He, then, may use the possessions, as Abraham, David, Job, and other wealthy people did.

When he sees a man who has no coat, he says to his money: "Come out, young Mr. Gulden! There is a poor naked man who has no coat; you must serve him. Over there lies a sick person who has no refreshment. Come forth, Sir Dollars! You must be on your way; go and help."

People who handle their possessions in this way are masters of their possessions. And, surely all honest Christians will do this.

Even if you should become rich justly and with God's help, do not depend on this either, and do not make mammon your god. Property is not given to you for you to build your trust on or boast about, all of which is vanity and nothing, but for you to use, enjoy, and share with others. Possessions belong in your hands, not in your heart.

> *"Now Abram was very rich in livestock,*
> *in silver, and in gold."*

The philosophers and the monks have often found fault with this passage and have wondered why the Holy Spirit records that Abraham was rich or greatly encumbered with the possession of cattle, silver, and gold. Both arrive at the opinion that so holy a man should not have had any wealth but should have lived in poverty, as befits someone who has put all his hope in the mercy of the one and only God, especially since he was an exile.

The philosophers indeed believed that they would achieve a great reputation if they disposed of their money and called themselves beggars. The monks did the same thing. Why is this? It is because they observe that through the use of wealth people generally become worse. Therefore they suppose that it would be advisable for them to condemn wealth and refrain from it altogether.

If it were a virtue to cast possessions away and be a beggar, Abraham would be praised without deserving it.

But now he keeps on managing and using his possessions, and his special effort is to keep his heart pure. He does not become proud because of his wealth and does not gain and preserve it in a greedy manner; but he is generous and hospitable.

"Blessed are the poor in spirit."

MATTHEW 5:3

But you say: "What? Must all Christians, then, be poor? Dare none of them have money, property, popularity, power, and the like? What are the rich to do? Must they surrender all their property and honor, or buy the kingdom of heaven from the poor?"

No. It does not say that whoever wants to have the kingdom of heaven must buy it from the poor. The command is to be "spiritually poor." Christ wants to discuss only the spiritual—how to live before God, above and beyond the external.

There is the example of David. He was an outstanding king, and he really had his wallet and treasury full of money, his barns full of grain, his land full of all kinds of goods and provisions. In spite of all this he had to be a poor beggar spiritually, as he sings of himself (Psalm 39:12): "I am poor, and a guest in the land." This is truly a heart that does not tie itself to property and riches.

The devil makes people weary and disgusted in giving their wealth to others. Because of ingratitude and malice nobody is willing to do any favors and to give any help. This is what the devil is looking for. When he sees that you want to do your neighbor a favor and to make good use of your money, he says: "I will spoil your good deed and make it sour!" This goes against nature, and thus love and kindness are suppressed even in the best and most prominent people. For it is a rare person indeed who can bear it if he does his best for country and people and gets nothing in return but shameful ingratitude, hatred, and envy.

That is what the devil is trying to achieve. He wants to tear you away from what is good and to make you like the world in its wickedness.

[Luther wrote the following to a woman who had given money for scholarships for students of theology at Wittenberg University.]

I wish you to know that your charitable gifts have, praise God, been very well spent and have helped, and continue to help, many poor students. I have no doubt that God, who prompted you to do this excellent thing, openly shows that he is well pleased with your thank offering, by means of which you confess and praise the grace which he has manifested to you in his dear Son, Jesus Christ. May God strengthen you in steadfast faith and perform the good work he has begun in you until the day of Jesus Christ. Amen.

A Christian ought to think: "Although I am unworthy and condemned, my God has given me in Christ all the riches of righteousness and salvation without any merit on my part, out of pure, free mercy, so that from now on I need nothing except faith which believes that this is true. Why should I not therefore freely, joyfully, with all my heart, and with an eager will do all things which I know are pleasing and acceptable to such a Father who has overwhelmed me with his inestimable riches? I will therefore give myself as a Christ to my neighbor, just as Christ offered himself to me. I will do nothing in this life except what I see is necessary, profitable, and salutary to my neighbor, since through faith I have an abundance of all good things in Christ."

But you might ask, "Why does God not do it all by himself, since he is able to help everyone and knows how to help everyone?" Yes, he can do it; but he does not want to do it alone. He wants us to work with him. He does us the honor of wanting to effect his work with us and through us. Although he alone is blessed, he does us the honor of wanting to share his blessedness with us.

Assurance in Death

Death was ever present in medieval times through the plague and other diseases, childbirth, war, and violence. Martin Luther wrote and preached on the subject to give comfort to Christians. He wrote letters of consolation to friends who had lost loved ones and to a congregation whose pastor was murdered. He spoke of his compassionate understanding of suicide. He understood Christ's merciful care at the time of sudden death. While he could rejoice in the knowledge of eternal life, he was well aware of the pain death caused to loved ones left behind. Luther's hymns speak of the certainty we can have of Christ's help in life and his receiving us into eternal life.

Since death is called a sleep, we know that we shall not remain in it; but we shall awake and live again, and the time during which we sleep cannot be long. It will seem as if we had just dropped off, so that we shall rebuke ourselves for having been appalled and frightened at so fine a sleep in the hour of death. And so from grave and corruption we shall in a moment go to meet our Lord and Savior Christ in the clouds. We shall be alive, entirely sound and vigorous, with a clean, bright transfigured body.

We should, therefore, with all confidence and joy commit and commend our soul, body, and life to Christ, as to our faithful Savior and Redeemer, even as we must, without all care, commit our life to him in bodily sleep and rest, certain that we shall not lose it, as it seems, but, kept safely and well in his hand, it will be sustained and restored to us.

[To Nicholas Hausmann, a close friend of Luther.]

My little John [two years old] thanks you, excellent Nicholas, for the rattle. He is very proud of it, and delighted with it.

My baby daughter, little Elizabeth [eight months old], has passed away. It is amazing what a sick, almost woman-like heart she has left to me, so much has grief for her overcome me. Never before would I have believed that a father's heart could have such tender feelings for his child. Do pray to the Lord for me.

[Luther saw the devil's part in suicide. We might see sickness or evil as a combatant today.]

I am not inclined to think that those who take their own lives are surely damned. My reason is that they do not do this of their own accord but are overcome by the power of the devil, like a person who is murdered by a robber in the woods.

[Luther wrote to his close friend and colleague, Philip Melanchthon.]

My father's death has certainly thrown me into sadness, thinking not only of the bonds of nature, but also of the very kind love my father had for me; for through him my Creator has given me all that I am and have. Even though it does comfort me that my father, strong in faith in Christ, has gently fallen asleep, yet the pity of heart and the memory of the most loving dealings with him have shaken me in the innermost parts of my being. Seldom if ever have I despised death as much as I do now.

Since I am now too sad, I am writing no more; for it is right and God-pleasing for me, as a son, to mourn such a father, from whom the Father of all mercies has brought me forth, and through whose sweat the Creator has fed and raised me to whatever I am now.

Beloved Jonas:

I have been so completely prostrated by the unexpected calamity which has befallen you that I do not know what to write. We have all sustained a loss in the death of your wife, the dearest companion of your life.

How you feel I can easily imagine from the effect that her death has had on me. Consolation is not to be found in the flesh at such time as this. One must find it in the spirit, in the realization that she has gone on before us to the Lord who has called us all and who in his good time will take us from the misery and wickedness of this world unto himself. Amen.

You have good cause to mourn. But I pray that when you mourn you will be mindful of our common Christian lot: that although parting is very bitter according to the flesh, yet in the life beyond we shall be reunited and gathered in sweetest communion with Christ who so loved us that he secured eternal life for us with his own blood and death. "If we be dead with him, we shall also live with him," as Saint Paul says [2 Timothy 2:11]. And it is well with us as long as we fall asleep with the sure confidence in the Son of God. This means truly that God's goodness and mercy extend beyond this life.

When we are brought to life on the last day, we shall spit on ourselves and say, "Fie on you for not having been bolder in believing on Christ, since the glory is so great!"

[A young pastor friend was murdered, bringing grief to his parishioners and to Luther. A letter of consolation to the people urged that the criminals be apprehended but also that the people not seek revenge but pray for the murderers.]

I beg you and exhort you, my dear friends, to do as Christ did and leave this disturbing matter, which rightly pains and grieves you so, to him who is the just Judge, as Saint Peter teaches us [1 Peter 2:23]. Take care that you do not become hostile to anyone because of it, or engender hatred or spread evil gossip, or curse and desire revenge. You would do wrong to be so hard-hearted as not to be stirred by this murder, or if you acceded to it and did not wholeheartedly condemn it. It would be equally wrong to curse the murderers, desire revenge, or nurse hostility rather than pray for them. We should condemn and punish such misdeeds and pray for recompense against Satan and his kingdom, so that the kingdom of Christ may be increased.

But we are to have mercy on these persons and, so long as there is hope that they may come to know and to better themselves, pray that God may mercifully enable them to repent of their murder and evil. We could not be helped by their condemnation but would greatly rejoice if they would be saved through our prayers and kindness.

In God's purpose this world is only a preparation and scaffolding for the life of the world to come.

"I will raise them up on the last day."
JOHN 6:54

The expression "raise up" is deliberately chosen here. It is of great significance. Otherwise it might offend us to hear Christ say: "Whoever believes in me shall have [everlasting life]" and then to discover that death, accompanied by many perils, comes nevertheless. Death is too evident and apparent. This moves our reason, mind and senses to fear deception in these words because we see the opposite before our very eyes.

Therefore Christ employs these words here to encourage us to be constant, to be strong, and to be of good cheer. It is as though Christ were saying: "Even though death tramples you underfoot and destroys you, I will still keep you; for I am your life and your true food which preserves you. Thus I will nourish you well, so that you live forever. Therefore do not worry. I will raise you up again, so that all will see and bear witness that you live."

Since everyone must depart, we must turn our eyes to God, to whom the path of death leads and directs us. Here we find the beginning of the narrow gate and of the straight path to life [Matthew 7:14]. All must joyfully venture forth on this path, for though the gate is quite narrow, the path is not long. Just as an infant is born with peril and pain from the small abode of its mother's womb into this immense heaven and earth, that is, into this world, so a person departs this life through the narrow gate of death. And although the heavens and the earth in which we dwell at present seem large and wide to us, they are nevertheless much narrower and smaller than the mother's womb in comparison with the future heaven.

The glory of Christ is still a veiled knowledge, like a thick cloud over the bright sun. For no one's heart can hold it and no one's understanding can comprehend that the glory is so great, especially as Christ now, in his Christians, appears so different.

But there, in the world to come, another light will shine, so that we shall no longer hold it only in faith and in the preaching and teaching of the word, but we shall see it all radiant before our eyes and shall look upon it with unspeakable and eternal joy.

Behold, thus we must learn to regard and to know our Lord Christ: not as One who helps us only with his teaching and example, and has now departed from us like the other saints, but as the One who is and remains constantly at our side and within us, particularly in the hour when this life comes to an end, and who is so close that he alone is in our hearts. This happens when I believe staunchly in him as the Savior who has passed through death unto the Father for me, in order to take me there too. Then I am on the right Way.

For this walking is nothing but a constant growth in faith and in an ever-stronger assurance of eternal life in Christ. If I persist in this faith and death attacks me and throws me down, if it chokes me in my prime or takes me by sword or fire and takes away all my five senses, then the journey is over, and I am already at my destination as I leap into yonder life.

[Verse 3 of Luther's hymn, "Lord, Keep Us Steadfast in Your Word."]

O Comforter of priceless worth,
Send peace and unity on earth;
Support us in our final strife
And lead us out of death to life.

Assurance for the Family

*M*artin Luther knew how busy family life could be, and he sometimes spoke of households rather than families. In his times, a household might be an extended family including single relatives, orphaned children of relatives, and other unrelated people. This was so in Martin and Katie Luther's busy household.

Luther speaks of the forgiveness needed in the home— one must know "how to close an eye" to some things in order to live peaceably. He wrote on the duties of children, young and old, toward their parents and that of parents toward their children.

The church also is family for a person, and Luther wrote tenderly of the comfort the Trinity can bring, perhaps being family to a person alone.

He understood, too, the plight of a Christian parent with non-Christian children, comforted these parents and spoke boldly of prayer. Luther's loving concern for people and his confidence in God shows in his writings on family.

The Christian church is your mother, who gives birth to you and bears you through the word. And this is done by the Holy Spirit, who bears witness concerning Christ.

In domestic and political economy the rule must be that one does not want anything done that is wrong. But if it is done, it must be met with the forgiveness of sins; otherwise one spoils things. Married people must close their eyes to many things in spouse and children, and yet order must not be neglected.

Therefore, this statement is true: The one who does not know how to close an eye does not know how to rule. This is gentleness. One must put up with much and yet not pass over everything.

A pious child will think thus: See here! If it did not seem improper to the Supreme Majesty that such a person should be my parent, why should it seem improper to me? If it pleased the Supreme God to fashion me in them, why should it displease me that I have been made or created in them? Therefore I shall venerate the workshop of my God, who has fashioned me. I shall not turn my eyes on the poverty, homeliness, and lowliness of my parents, but on God, the Workman.

You see, in this way reverence flows from God to the parents and does not originate in them. They are looked upon as being more than mere flesh and blood, as being the workshop of the Supreme Majesty.

If we want qualified and capable people for both civil spiritual leadership, we must spare no effort, time, and expense in teaching and educating our children to serve God and humankind. We must not think only of amassing money and property for them. God can provide for them and make them rich without our help, as indeed he does daily. But he has given and entrusted children to us with the command that we train and govern them according to his will. Otherwise God would have no need of father and mother.

Therefore let all people know that it is their chief duty to bring up their children in the fear and knowledge of God, and if the children are gifted to give them opportunity to learn and study so that they may be of service wherever they are needed.

If obedience is not rendered in the homes, we shall never have a whole city, country, principality, or kingdom well governed. For this order in the homes is the first rule; it is the source of all other rule and government.

For what is a city but a group of homes? How is an entire city to be well governed if there is no order in the homes, nay, if child, servant, and maid are disobedient there? Likewise, what is an entire country but a group of cities, villages, and hamlets? If the homes are badly governed, how can an entire country be well governed?

Children are to be rebuked or chastised in love. Parents are not to vent their furious temper on them, unconcerned about the way to correct the error of their children. For when the spirit has been cowed, one is of no use for anything and despairs of everything, is timid in doing and undertaking everything. And, what is worse, this timidity, implanted during the tender years, can almost never thereafter be eradicated. For since they have learned to be frightened at every word of their parents, they are subsequently afraid of even a rustling leaf of a tree.

Those nursemaids, too, should be checked who at nightfall terrify children with frightening forms and gestures. With the greatest care a child should be trained to have the right fear, to fear what is to be feared, but not to be timid. Some parents are satisfied if only their children are timid. But this is very harmful for later life.

This is the church of the saints, the new creation of God, our brothers, sisters, and our friends, in whom we see nothing but blessing and nothing but consolation, though not always with the eyes of the flesh but with the eyes of the spirit. Whose heart will not be lifted up, even in the midst of great evils, when they believe the very truth, namely that the blessings of all the saints are their blessings?

Thus we can truthfully apply to ourselves the words Elisha spoke to his fearful servants, "'Fear not, for those who are with us are more numerous that those with them.' And Elisha prayed and said, 'Lord, open the eyes of the young man that he may see.' And the Lord opened his eyes and he saw. And behold, the mountain was full of horses and chariots of fire around Elisha (2 Kings 6:16-17)."

All that remains for us now is to pray that our eyes, that is the eyes of our faith, may be opened that we may see the church around us.

If a Christian spouse should have grown children with a non-Christian mate (as often happened in the days of the apostle Paul) and the children should not want to be baptized or become Christians, then, inasmuch as no one should be forced to believe but only willingly be drawn by God through his gospel, the father and mother should not abandon the children or withdraw or fail in their motherly or fatherly duties. Parents do not sin and pollute themselves in unbelieving children. But they should guide and care bodily for these children as though they were the holiest of Christians. For they are not impure or unholy, Paul says; that is, your faith can demonstrate itself in them and thus remain pure and holy.

So it should be done now and at all times. Where children do not want to accept the gospel, one should not therefore leave them or send them away but care for them and support them like the best of all Christians, commending their faith to God, so long as they are obedient and upright in all other things having to do with outward living.

"Jesus answered him,
'Those who love me will keep my word, and my
Father will love them, and we will come to them
and make our home with them.'"

JOHN 14:23

God and a Christian will cleave unto each other as friends, for the Holy Spirit prepares the human heart and consecrates it as a holy house and dwelling, a temple and dwelling-place of God. What a glorious, noble, loving, and precious guest and house-companion does one receive—God the Father and the Son and certainly with them also the Holy Spirit!

God accomplishes much through the faith and longing of another, even a stranger, even though there is still no personal faith. This is given through the channel of another's intercession, as in the gospel Christ raised the widow's son at Nain because of the prayers of his mother apart from the faith of the son. And he freed the little daughter of the Canaanite woman from the demon through the faith of the mother apart from the daughter's faith.

For Christ has never rejected a single person who was brought to him through someone else's faith, but accepted all.

[Many people came to Martin Luther for marriage counseling. After a particularly busy time he wrote the following to a friend.]

What a bother these matrimonial cases are to us! It takes great effort and labor to get couples together. Afterward it requires even more pains to keep them together. The fall of Adam so corrupted human nature that it is very fickle. It is as inconstant as quicksilver.

Adam and Eve must have scolded each other roundly during their nine hundred years together. Eve would have said, "You ate the apple!" And Adam would have replied, "But why did you give it to me?" There is no doubt that during their long life they encountered numberless evils as they sighed over their fall. It must have been an extraordinary regime!

[Luther gave a sentence that could be used as a family or household prayer.]

Lord, grant that anger or other bitterness does not reign over us, but that by your grace, genuine kindness, loyalty, and every kind of friendliness, generosity, and gentleness may reign in us. Amen.

Assurance in Aging

For Martin Luther there was no time in life when we could not be involved in some sort of work to give glory to God and to help other people. And there is no time in life when we should not have our eyes fixed on the blessed hope of eternal life with God. This hope gives us endurance for life now and the assurance of God's great love for us always.

Through the gospel we have been given a treasure which is not goods and gold, power and honor, joy and happiness of this world. It is not even life on this earth, but hope, a living and blessed hope. This hope will quicken us into life and blessedness in body and soul, perfectly and eternally. To this treasure the gospel calls us. In this treasure we are baptized. Therefore let us live this earthly life bearing in mind that we shall leave it behind, and let us stretch out after that blessed hope and await it at all times.

But how long shall we wait for that blessed hope? Will it remain but a hope for ever, and will it never be fulfilled? No, Saint Paul says, our blessed hope will not always remain a hope. It will eventually be made manifest, so that we shall no longer only hope and wait for it, but what we now believe and hope for will then be made manifest in us. We shall possess with full certainty what we now await. But meanwhile we must wait for that blessed hope until it be revealed.

This transitory life we have unceasingly before our eyes, we think about it and care for it, but we turn our back toward the everlasting life. Day and night we pursue this earthly life, but the eternal life we throw to the winds.

But this should certainly not be so with Christians; rather the opposite should obtain. Christians should look at this temporal life with closed or blinking eyes, but they should look at the future eternal life with eyes wide open and in clear bright light. A Christian should have only the left hand in this life here on earth. But with the right hand, with the soul, and with the whole heart the Christian should be in the other life, in heaven, and should wait for it always with certain hope and a joyful mind.

"I pray that, according to the riches of his glory, he may grant that you may be strengthened in your inner being with power through his Spirit."

EPHESIANS 3:16

Worldly people are full of courage and of high spirits, and so are Christians. Christians are much stronger through the Holy Spirit, for they fear neither the world nor the devil, neither death nor misfortune. This is called spiritual strength. For the little word "spirit" rightly means courage, which is bold and daring. For spiritual strength is not the flesh and bones, but the heart and courage itself.

Therefore Saint Paul says: "This is what I desire and pray for you from God, that he may give you such a strong and daring mind, such a powerful and joyful spirit, as fears no shame, poverty, sin, devil, and death, that you will be certain that nothing can harm you and that you will not want."

Worldly courage endures no longer than there is some earthly good on which to rely. But the true courage trusts in God alone and has no other good or gold than

God alone. In him it withstands all evil and wins an altogether different heart and courage from that of the world.

Every age in life and place in life has enough good works to do for God and neighbor without needing to look for strange ones.

God, to whom I cried, fills my heart through his eternal word and Spirit in the midst of trouble so that I hardly feel it. For we must not suppose that God comforts us without means and without his word in our hearts. This does not happen without the external word. The Holy Spirit well knows how to remind us of this word in our hearts and how to stir it up, although we may have heard it fully ten years ago.

What could be more pleasing to God and more benefi-
cial to other people than so to live in your calling that
God is thereby honored and that by your example you
bring others to love God's word and to praise his name?
Likewise, what virtues are more useful in the whole life of
a Christian than modesty, meekness, patience, and living
in harmony with people?

We must not seek to build for ourselves eternal life here in this world and pursue it and cleave to it as if it were our greatest treasure and heavenly kingdom, and as if we wished to exploit the Lord Christ and the gospel and achieve wealth and power through him.

No, but because we have to live on earth, and so long as it is God's will, we should eat, drink, woo, plant, build, and have house and home and what God grants. We use them as guests and strangers in a strange land, who know they must leave all such things behind and take our staff out of this strange land and evil, unsafe inn, homeward bound for our true fatherland where there is nothing but security, peace, rest, and joy for evermore.

This life is not a state of being righteous, but rather, of growth in righteousness;

> not a state of being healthy, but a period of healing;
> not a state of being, but becoming;
> not a state of rest, but of exercise and activity.

We are not yet what we shall be, but we grow toward it;
> the process is not yet finished, but is still going on;
> this life is not the end, it is the way to a better life.

All does not yet shine with glory; nevertheless, all is being purified (2 Corinthians 3:18).

If you young fellows were wise, the devil couldn't do anything to you; but since you aren't wise, you need us who are old. If old people were strong and young people were wise it would be worth something.

I, out of my own experience, am able to witness, that Jesus Christ is true God; I know full well and have found what the name of Jesus has done for me.

Indeed, for what purpose do we older folks exist, other than to care for, instruct, and bring up the young? It is utterly impossible for these foolish young people to instruct and protect themselves. This is why God has entrusted them to us who are older and know from experience what is best for them. This is also why Moses commands in Deuteronomy 32[:7], "Ask your father and he will tell you; your elders, and they will show you."

*"Do not say, 'Why were the former
days better than these?' For it is not from
wisdom that you ask this."*

ECCLESIASTES 7:10

This is how the human heart customarily complains whenever it experiences the ingratitude of the world. "Things are worse than they used to be." But you, do not talk this way, for you are not asking or arguing the right way. Old people usually speak this way: "When I was a child, everything was better." They are what the poet calls "glorifiers of times past."

But this Scripture says: "This is false; things were never right." The reason you see and understand this only now is that as we grow, our experiences of things and our occasions to be angry grow also. A boy does not care and is not moved when someone cheats or murders someone else, but goes on playing, hunting, and riding. To his mind the highest of crimes is when someone steals another's marbles, and this makes him angry. But when he becomes the head of a household, then he is sensitive to the annoyance and unfaithfulness of his household, and he becomes angry if a horse breaks a leg or an ox is not properly fattened.

Therefore the world has always been evil, but we have not always been in the world and are not now. When we were children, nothing disturbed us; we ourselves did indeed lead a more peaceful life, but the world has always been the same. See to it, then, that you have a peaceful and tranquil heart and that you do not get angry when you see this evil. You will never change the world, but see to it that you change into another kind of person.

Assurance of Salvation

Christ, Luther says, "is the Cause and Leader" of our salvation. Through Christ we are saved from sin, death, and the devil (or power of evil). It is the unfathomable love God has for us in Christ that draws us to him.

Because of Christ's life, death, and resurrection we have life with Christ now and forever. This is God's amazing, incomprehensible love for us.

Whenever you consider the doctrine of justification and wonder how or where or in what condition to find a God who justifies or accepts sinners, then you must know there is no other God than this man Jesus Christ. Take hold of him; cling to him with all your heart, and spurn all speculation about the Divine Majesty. For whoever investigates the majesty of God will be consumed by his glory. Christ himself says, "I am the Way" (John 14:6).

That is why the apostle Paul makes such a frequent practice of linking Jesus Christ with God the Father, to teach us what is the true Christian religion. It does not begin at the top, as all other religions do; it begins at the bottom. You must run directly to the manger and the mother's womb, embrace this Infant and Virgin's Child in your arms, and look at him—born, being nursed, growing up, going about in human society, teaching, dying, rising again, ascending above all the heavens, and having authority over all things.

"For Jesus is the one who leads them to salvation."
HEBREWS 2:10 (TEV)

Christ is the Cause and Leader of salvation, for God
draws and leads his children to glory through him. One
would commonly say that Christ is the Instrument and
the Means by which God leads his children. For God does
not compel believers to salvation by force and fear, but by
this pleasing spectacle of his mercy and love he moves
and draws through love all whom he will save.

Repeatedly in the Gospels, Christ declares that he was sent by the Father. He says and does nothing of his own accord, but states that it is the Father's order and command to all the world to believe Christ as God himself.

Therefore it is certain that those who bypass the Person of Christ never find the true God. Since God is fully in Christ, where he places himself for us, no effort to deal with God without and apart from Christ on the strength of human thoughts and devotions will be successful.

Those who would travel the right road and not go astray with their faith, let them begin where God says and where God wants to be found, in this man—Jesus Christ.

"When the goodness and loving kindness of God our Savior appeared he saved us, not because of any works of righteousness that we had done, but according to his mercy, through the water of rebirth and renewal by the Holy Spirit."

TITUS 3:4-5

Our salvation is given us at once and is not obtained by works. For birth does not produce one member only, a hand or a foot, but the entire life, a complete human being, who is not active in order to be born but is born in order to be active.

Just so works do not make us clean and pious. Nor do they save us; but first we are made clean and pious and are saved. Then we freely perform works to the glory of God and the benefit of our neighbor.

Those who are saved still feel evil inclinations. You can understand this from a parable in Luke 10:34ff concerning the man who went down from Jerusalem to Jericho and fell among the murderers, who beat him and left him half-dead. Later the Samaritan attended to him, bound up his wounds, looked after him, and had him cared for.

Here you see that since this man is now being cared for, he is no longer mortally ill but is now sure to live. Only one thing is lacking: he is not completely well. Life is there, but he does not yet have perfect health but is still in the care of the physicians. He must continue to be cared for.

Thus we also have the Lord Christ completely and are certain of eternal life. Nevertheless, we do not yet enjoy perfect health. Something of the old Adam still remains in the flesh.

[Martin Luther's hymn "Dear Christians, One and All" speaks very personally of Luther's understanding of salvation. The ten-verse hymn has been called a "ballad of the believer's justification."]

But God had seen my wretched state
    Before the world's foundation,
    And, mindful of his mercies great,
    He planned for my salvation.
    He turned to me a father's heart;
    He did not choose the easy part,
    But gave his dearest treasure.

God said to his beloved Son:

  " 'Tis time to have compassion.
    Then go, bright jewel of my crown,
    And bring to all salvation;
    From sin and sorrow set them free;
    Slay bitter death for them that they
    May live with you forever."

O death, where is thy sting? O grave, where is thy victory? This is so true that even Satan cannot deny it. Christ's resurrection and victory over sin, death and hell is greater than all heaven and earth. You can never imagine his resurrection and victory so great but that in actuality it is far, far greater. For as his person is mighty, eternal, without limit, incomprehensible, so also is his resurrection, victory and triumph mighty, eternal, without limit, incomprehensible. Were hell a thousand times more, and death ten thousand times more, it would be but a spark, a mere drop, compared with Christ's resurrection, victory and triumph.

Christ's resurrection, victory and triumph gives Christ to all who believe in him. Since we have been baptized in his name, and believe in him, it follows that even if you and I underwent sin, death and hell a hundred thousandfold, it would amount to nothing; for Christ's resurrection, victory and triumph, which have been given me in the baptism and in the word by faith, and therefore are my own, are infinitely greater. If this is true, and I most certainly believe it to be true, then let sin, death and hell dog my steps and growl at me. What will they do to us? What can they do? What?

Christ offered himself once for all, so that he is himself both Priest and Sacrifice, and the Altar is the Cross. There, then we have this High Priest, Jesus Christ, with his altar and offering, most shamefully treated by the Jews and soldiers. And yet he carries on his shoulders the sin of us all. There we lie, you and I and all people, from the first man Adam until the end of the world.

Acknowledgments

The Book of Concord. Theodore G. Tappert, ed. Philadelphia: Fortress Press, 1959.

Luther, Martin. *Daily Readings from Luther's Writings.* Barbara Owen, ed. Minneapolis: Augsburg Books, 1993.

Luther, Martin. *Daily Readings with Martin Luther.* James Atkinson, ed. Springfield, Ill.: Templegate Publishers, 1987.

Luther, Martin. *Day by Day We Magnify Thee.* Margarete Steiner and Percy Scott, eds. Philadelphia: Fortress Press, 1982.

Luther, Martin. *Great Thoughts From Luther.* Hilda Noel Schroetter, ed. London: William Collins Sons, n.d.

Luther, Martin. *Luther: Letters of Spiritual Counsel.* vol. XVIII. The Library of Christian Classics. Theodore G. Tappert, ed. Philadelphia: Westminster Press, 1955.

Luther, Martin. *The Table Talk of Martin Luther.* Thomas S. Kepler, ed. Grand Rapids: Baker Book House, 1979.

Lutheran Book of Worship. Minneapolis: Augsburg Fortress, 1978.

Luther's Works. American edition, Jaroslav Pelikan and Helmut Lehmann, eds. Philadelphia and St. Louis: Fortress Press and Concordia Publishing House, 1955–1986.

Sermons of Martin Luther, The Church Postils. John Nicholas Lenker, ed. Grand Rapids: Baker Books, 1995.

What Luther Says. Compiled by Ewald M. Plass. St. Louis: Concordia Publishing House, 1959.